KU-297-986

BEANObooks

JOKE BOOK

PaRragon

Bath · New York · Singapore · Hong Kong · Cologne · Delhi · Melbourne

BEANObooks

First published by Parragon in 2007
Parragon
Queen Street House
4 Queen Street
Bath BA1 1HE, UK

"The Beano" ® © and associated characters
TM © D.C. Thomson & Co., Ltd., 2007

All rights reserved. No part of this publication may be
reproduced, stored in a retrieval system or transmitted,
in any form or by any means, electronic, mechanical,
photocopying, recording or otherwise, without the prior
permission of the copyright holder.

ISBN 978-1-4054-8747-4

Printed in England

Why did the dinosaur cross the road?

Because chickens hadn't been invented yet!

Where do dinosaurs wear ties?

Around their tyrannosaurus necks!

What do you get if you cross Gnasher with an elephant?

A very nervous postman!

Dad: Dennis – If you had ten sweets and Walter asked for one, how many sweets would you have?

Dennis: Ten sweets!

Dennis: What's stripy and green with horrible hairy legs, big bulging eyes and sharp looking teeth?

Walter: I don't know.

Dennis: Nor do I – but one's just gone down your jumper!

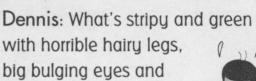

Sir: We only have half a day of school this morning.

Danny: Hurrah!

Sir: We'll have the other half this afternoon!

Sir: Danny, can you name an animal that lives in the jungle?

Danny: An elephant.

Sir: Good, now can you name another one?

Danny: Another elephant!

What is black and white and black and white and black and white?

A penguin rolling down a hill!

What is black and white and red at the top?

A sunburnt penguin!

What is black and white and red at the bottom?

A sunburnt penguin standing on its head!

What do you call a boy with a spade on his head?

Doug!

What do you call a boy *without* a spade on his head?

Doug-less!

Dennis: If I have 50p in one pocket and 75p in the other pocket, what have I got?

Walter's trousers!

Walter: How many eggs does it take to make a stink bomb?

Dennis: Quite a phew!

Walter: What game is the smelliest to play?

Dennis: Ping-pong!

Why do elephants all have grey trunks?

Because they're all on the same swimming team!

What would you get if you crossed an elephant with a kangaroo?

Great big holes in Australia!

What has four legs and goes oom oom?

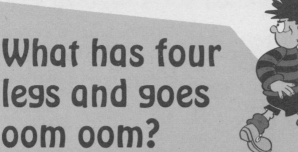

A cow walking backwards!

What has four legs and goes oow oow?

A cow in Australia!

What was wrong with wooden cars?

They wooden go!

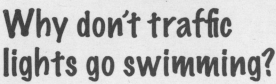

Why don't traffic lights go swimming?

Because they take forever to change!

What do you get if you sit under a cow?
A pat on the head!

What films do cows like best?
Moo-*sicals*

15

What's the difference between a **cat** and a **frog**? A cat has **nine** lives, but a frog croaks **every night!**

What did the frog order at the fast food restaurant? French **flies** and a diet **croak!**

Dennis: **Why are Softies like Cinderella?**

Gnasher: *Because they're always running away from the ball!*

What's the difference between HOMEWORK and BREAKFAST?

Gnasher didn't eat Dennis's Breakfast!

Why did Curly eat Dennis's homework?

Because Gnasher wasn't hungry!

Why was the centipede angry?

He was tired of people pulling his leg, leg, leg, leg…!

What animal flies around the jungle?

A hot air baboon!

Walter: Doctor! Doctor! I feel like a fishing net with a hole in it!

Doctor: Don't worry – it isn't catching!

Walter: Doctor! Doctor! I feel dizzy and my head's spinning!

Doctor: Yes – there's a lot of that going around!

Dennis: Do you want to hear the joke about the rare disease?

Walter: Yes please!

Dennis: What's the point - *you'll never get it!*

Dennis: Do you want to hear the joke about the dustbin?

Walter: Is it good?

Dennis: No - *it's Rubbish!*

Dennis: What's big and grey and has four wheels?

An elephant on a skateboard!

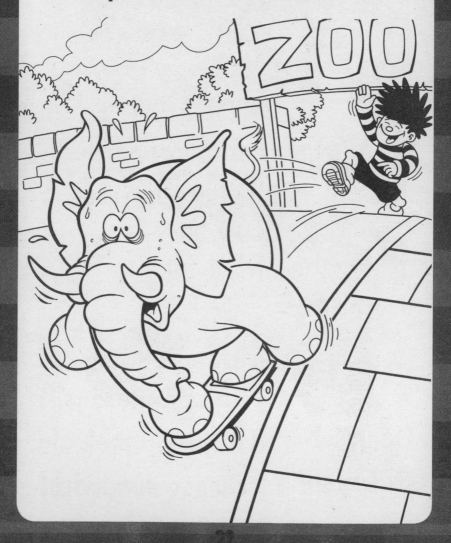

What's yellow and dangerous?
Shark infested custard!

What's green and dangerous?
An angry lettuce!

What's yellow, green and brown and dangerous?
A three-week old cheese sandwich!

What do you get if you cross a teacher with a vampire?

Lots of blood tests!

What is the scariest insect?

A zom-bee!

How do you know when you've got a hippo in your fridge?

Footprints in the butter!

How do you get an elephant into a fridge?

Ask the hippo to move over!

Why shouldn't you eat green elephants?

Because they're not ripe yet!

What is grey and squirts jam at you?

An elephant eating a doughnut!

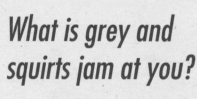

Where do cows go on holiday?
Moo York!

Where do pigs go on holiday?
Ham-sterdam!

Where do great big hairy gorillas go on holiday?
Anywhere they want to!

27

What's the last thing that goes through a fly's mind when it hits a windscreen?

Its **bottom!**

How do you know which end of a worm is its head?

Wait for it to **burp!**

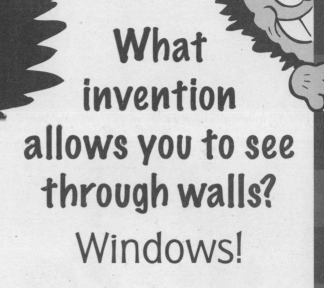

What invention allows you to see through walls?
Windows!

What colour is a burp?
Burple!

Dennis: How do you get three softies in a tree?

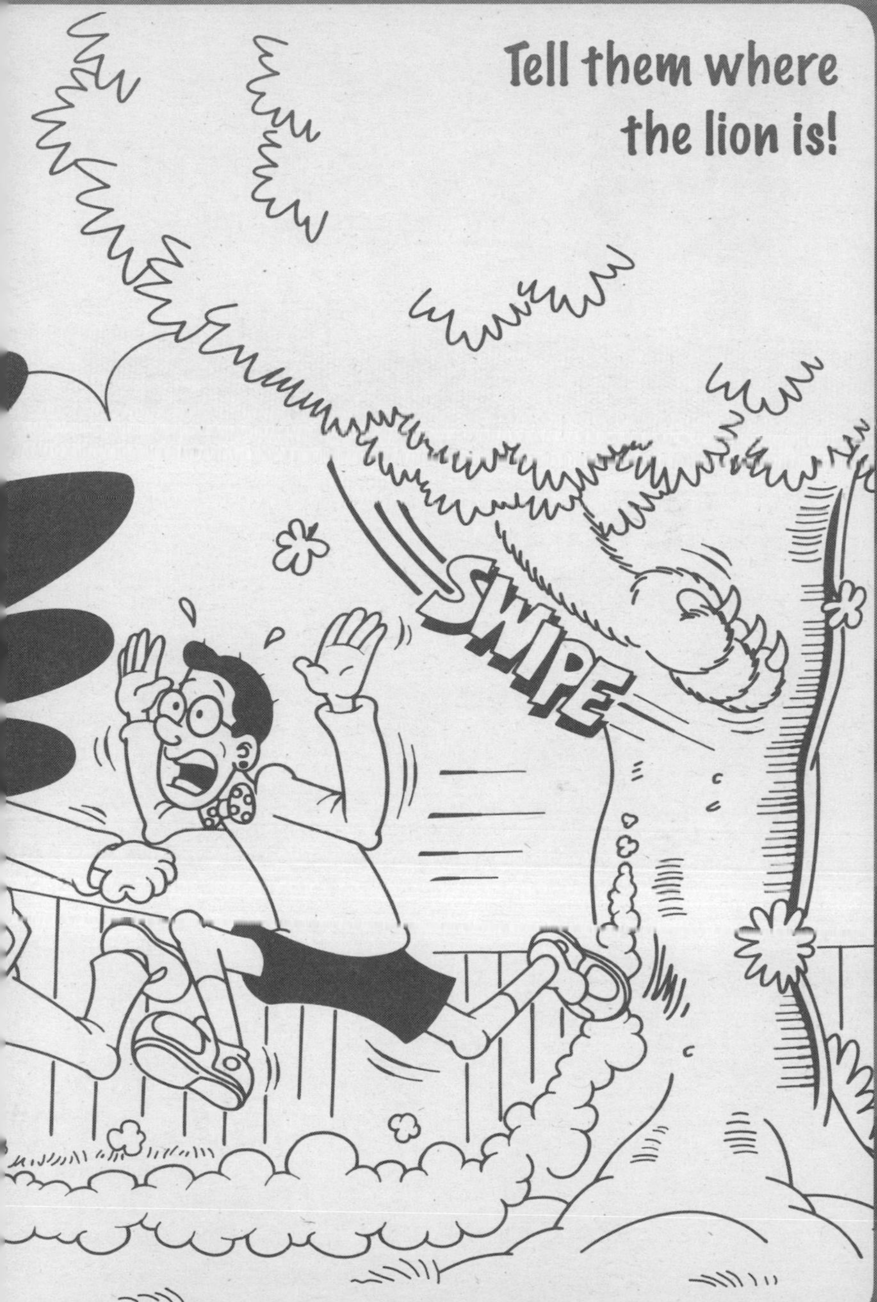
Tell them where the lion is!
SWIPE

HOW DO SPACEMEN
TIE THEIR SHOELACES?

WITH
ASTRO-KNOTS!

How do fish tie
their shoelaces?

They don't have
shoelaces - they
only have **soles!**

HOW DOES ROBIN HOOD
TIE HIS SHOELACES?
WITH **A BOW!**

What has **20** feet and sounds awful?

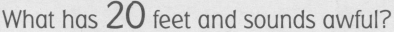

The school choir!

What has a Q
and lots of Ps
and smells awful?
School dinners!

Dennis: Can you get in trouble for something you didn't do?

Head: No, Dennis.

Dennis: Great! I didn't do my homework!

Head: Who invented fireplaces?

Dennis: Alfred the Grate!

What do you get if you cross a lawnmower with a budgie?

Shredded tweet!

Where do you send a kangaroo to get glasses?

A hoptician!

Dennis: **Doctor! Doctor! I think I've turned into Gnasher!**

Doctor: **Sit down and tell me all about it.**

Dennis: **I can't - I'm not allowed on the furniture!**

Walter: Are you sure there aren't any sharks?

Dennis: Don't worry! The crocodiles ate all the sharks!

What kind of coffee do vampires drink?

De-*coffinated*!

What did the witch ask for at the hotel?

Broom-service!

What do you get if you cross a cow with an earthquake?

A milkshake!

What do you get if you cross a stupid cow with an earthquake?

A <u>thick</u> milkshake!

KNOCK★ KNOCK★

Who's there?

I wasn't

I wasn't who?

I wasn't knocking I was playing football against your door!

KNOCK★ KNOCK★ CRASH★★★

Who's there?

It wasn't

It wasn't who?

It wasn't me who missed the door and broke your window!

How did
the three bears keep
their house safe?
They fitted **Goldi-locks**!

How did the fast food restaurant keep their French fries safe?
They had a *burger* alarm!

What do giraffes have that other animals don't have?

Baby giraffes!

Why don't grasshoppers play football?

They prefer **cricket**!

HOW MANY SOFTIES DOES IT TAKE TO CHANGE A

LIGHT BULB?

NONE.
Softies don't change
light bulbs, they get their
mumsies to do it for them!

HOW MANY GNASHERS DOES IT TAKE TO CHANGE A

LIGHT BULB?

NONE.
Who do you think broke it in the first place?

What do you call a boy with a plank on his head?
Ed-wood!

What do you call a boy with a seagull on his head?
Cliff!

Why do rabbits chew carrots?

Because sucking them would take ages!

Why do rabbits have long ears?

Because if they had long necks they'd be giraffes!

What is a butcher's favourite dog?

A sausage dog!

What is a baker's favourite dog?

A Great Danish!

What is a greengrocer's favourite dog?

A collie!

KNOCK! KNOCK!

Who's there?

The engineer.

The engineer who?

The engineer who came to fix your doorbell!

KNOCK! KNOCK!

Who's there?

The engineer again.

The engineer again who?

The engineer again who came to fix your doorbell, but the door seems to be working!

What goes Moo-chew-pop! Moo-chew-pop!?

A cow eating bubblegum!

What goes Oink-oink-ouch! Oink-oink-ouch!?

A pig eating stinging nettles!

How did the teacher know that Smiffy had copied Danny's answers?

On question five Danny wrote "I don't know" and Smiffy wrote "Me neither!"

What do you call someone who keeps on talking when no one is listening?

A teacher!

What insect robs banks?
A *baddy*-long-legs!

What insect robs small banks?
A baddy-*short*-legs!

What insect robs banks but always gets caught?
A baddy-*no*-legs!

Minnie: *Dad! I think this violin is broken!*

Dad: *Well stop blowing it then!*

Dennis: Dad! - I think my alarm clock is made of cheese!

Dad: Why's that?

Dennis: It keeps going off!

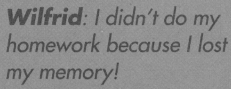

Wilfrid: I didn't do my homework because I lost my memory!

Teacher: How did that happen, Wilfrid?

Wilfrid: How did what happen?

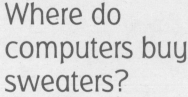

Where do computers buy sweaters?

On the interknit!

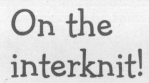

What
do you
call a fly with
no wings?
A walk!

What has
100 legs
but can't
walk?

Fifty pairs
of trousers!

What do you give a butterfly with a sore throat?

Antiseptic **moth** wash!

What do you give an ant with a sore throat?

Anti-septic!

Why do dogs have fur coats?
Because they'd look silly in dresses!

What do you call a dinosaur
that is always on time?

A pronto-saurus!

What do you get if you cross
a pig with a dinosaur?

Jurassic pork!

What do you call a broken boomerang?

A stick!

What's brown and sticky?

A stick!

What looks like a stick, smells like a stick but isn't a stick?

A stick. *I lied about the last bit!*

Did you hear the one about the ship full of yo-yos that hit a rock?

It sunk 37 times!

How many rude people does it take to change a light bulb?
None of your business!!!

What do you call a recycled wasp?
A used-to-bee!

What do you call a recycled earwig?
An earwigo-again!

What do you call
a French girl with
a cream bun
on her head?
E Clare!

What do you
call a girl with a
lawnmower on her head?
Mo!

What goes
99-thump, 99-thump,
99-thump?
*A centipede with a
wooden leg!*

What goes 99-thump-clunk-
clunk, 99-thump-clunk-clunk,
99-thump-clunk-clunk?
*A centipede with a wooden
leg and crutches!*

What goes
tring! tring!
whizz?
*A centipede with a
wooden leg riding
a bicycle!*

Curly: Hey, Dennis, what did you get the little cup for?

Dennis: Singing.

Curly: What did you get the big one for?

Dennis: Stopping!

Who grants
fish three
wishes?

The Fairy
Codmother!

What fish can fix pianos?

A Tuna fish!

What do you get if you cross Gnasher with a small parrot?
A budgerigrrrrrrrr!

Where can't you park in the jungle?
On the double yellow lions!

What do you give a sick pig?
Oinkment!

What do you give a sick parrot?
Tweetment!

How do you stop your nose from running?
Hide its trainers!

What do you get if you cross a giant mosquito with a computer?

A mega-*bite*!

How do chickens communicate?
By walky-**turkey**!

How do parrots communicate?
By **squawky**-talky!

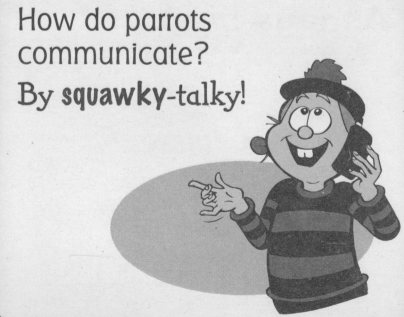

What's pink and wobbles? A jellybaby!

What's the difference between babies and football players? **One drools and the other dribbles!**

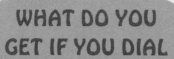

KNOCK! KNOCK!

Who's there?

Aitch.

Aitch who?

I'll como back when your cold is better!

KNOCK! KNOCK!

Who's there?

Tiss.

Tiss who?

Still got a cold then?

What dog prefers a mud bath?
Gnasher!

What's green and hangs from trees?

Monkey snot!

What's green and hangs from caves?

A sick bat!

Dennis: How do you keep a Softy in suspense?

Walter: I don't know....please tell me....oh, go on....tell me!...

What do you call two rows of cabbages?
A dual cabbageway!

Why do birds fly south in the winter?

BECAUSE THEY CAN'T AFFORD THE BUS FARE!

What's big and red and stands in the corner?

A naughty bus!

What's black and white and sneaky?

A zebra double crossing!

What's yellow and smells of bananas?
Monkey sick!

What lives in the sea and goes to the toilet eight times a day?

An octo-**poos**!

Where do all the old vampires live?

Gran-sylvania!

What does the abominable
snowman have for lunch?
Iceburgers!

What do sea monsters
have for lunch?
Fish and ships!

**What do vampires
have for lunch?**
Just a quick bite!

What's yellow on the inside and purple on the outside?

A banana in disguise!

What do you get if you put candles on a toilet?

A birthday potty!

Mum: Dennis, is your cough any better?

Dennis: Yes, Mum! I've been practising it all week!

What do you call a girl
with a tennis ball on
her head?

An-nette!

What do you call
a girl with one
leg shorter than
the other?

Ei-leen!

What's the difference between snot and sprouts?

Kids won't eat sprouts!

What sits in a bowl of custard looking cross?

Apple Grumble!

What do you get if you put Walter's favourite toy in the freezer?

A teddy-brrrrrr!

What do you get if you run over Walter's favourite toy with a lawnmower?

A shreddy-bear!

Why shouldn't you take a crocodile to the zoo?

Because they'd rather go to the cinema!

What is hairy and coughs?

A sick coconut!

What did the mummy balloon say to the baby balloon when she found him playing with a pin?

"You've let me down, you've let your father down and, worst of all, you've let yourself down!"

What do you call a
girl with a church
on her head?

ABBY!

What do you call a
girl with a draughty
church on her head?

ABI-GALE!

What do you call a
nervous witch?
A twitch!

What do short-sighted
ghosts wear?

Spook-tacles!

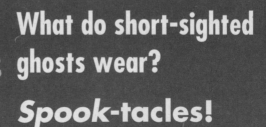

What's small, brown and fluffy?
A toffee that's been in your pocket for weeks!

What's brown, yellow and hairy?
Cheese on toast that fell on the carpet!

What is Walter's least favourite food?
Taglia-teddy!

Teacher: Plug, if you use this text book you will get your homework done in half the time.

Plug: Great! Can I have two?!

Teacher: Who invented fractions?

Plug: Henry the Eighth!

Why did the chicken cross the road?

No-one is *eggs*-actly sure!

Why did the second chicken cross the road?

He did it as a *yolk*!

What's the difference between Walter and Gnasher?

One wears silly clothes and the other just pants!

Do robots have brothers?
No, just tran-*sistors*!

What do you call a three-legged donkey?

A **wonkey**!

What bird stole the bath plug?

A **robber** duck!

Where do you find a
queue of bees?

At a **buzz** stop!

What goes Buzz-choo!
Buzz-choo?

A bee with a cold!

What's the best way of counting cows?

With a cow-culator!

What tool can help you with your sums?

4+4=

1x2=

3x2=

Multi-pliers!

What has six legs but can't run? Three Softies with their shoelaces tied together!

Dad: What did you learn at school today, Dennis?
Dennis: Not enough – I have to go back again tomorrow!

What do you get if you cross a plumber with a field full of cow pats?

The **Pooed** Piper!

What do you call a sheep with a parachute?

A woolly jumper!

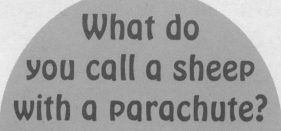

What do you call a sheep with a parachute that pushes in front of you?

A woolly queue jumper!

Where do you take a sick gnome?

To the **elf** centre!

How do you make fairy cakes?

With **elf**-raising flour!

Gnasher was tied to a rope in the garden but could still chase after Walter. How?

Because Dennis forgot to tie the rope to anything!

What do you get if you cross Gnasher with a mosquito?

A naughty gnome-sized gnat that gnoshes on all the neighbours!

What shoes do frogs wear?
Open-**toad** sandals!

What do clouds wear under their clothes?
Thunderwear!

What do you call a boy with a doorstep on his head?

Matt!

What do you call a boy with a cat on his head?

Claude!

What's a pirate's favourite pudding?

Jelly-Roger!

Why do sharks live in saltwater?

Because pepper makes them sneeze!

Dennis: Dad! There's something running across the bathroom floor and it's got no legs!

Dad: What are you talking about, Dennis?

Dennis: WATER!!!

Why did the bees
go on strike?

For more honey
and shorter flowers!

What is yellow and
black and always
complaining?
A **grumble**-bee!

What two vegetables do you find in the toilet?

Leeks and peas!

What has a bottom at the top?

Your legs!

What do you call a red,
flying dinosaur?

A *cherry*-dactyl!

What do you call
a dinosaur that
won't give up?

**A try, try,
try-ceratops!**

Walter: Doctor! Doctor! Danny thinks he's a lift!

Doctor: Well tell him to come in!

Walter: I can't. He doesn't stop at this floor!

Walter: Doctor! Doctor! I think I'm turning into a sheep!

Doctor: How do you feel?

Walter: Really baaaaaaad!

Why did the elephant paint the soles of it's feet yellow?

So it could hide upside down in a bowl of custard!

That's silly! I've never seen an elephant in a bowl of custard!

See! It works!

How do you spell 'hungry horse' using only four letters?

M.T.G.G!

How do you spell 'mouse trap' using only three letters?

C.A.T!

What's a mouse's favourite game?

Hide and **squeak** !

What is a cat's favourite breakfast?

Mice crispies!

What are Dennis and Gnasher's favourite chocolates?

Softy-centres!

Teacher: Danny, can you name six things with milk in them?

Danny: Cheese, butter and four cows!

Danny: I've added up these sums ten times!

Teacher: Good work, Danny.

Danny: And here are my ten answers!

KNOCK! KNOCK!

Who's there?

Want.

Want who?

Good - now try counting to three!

KNOCK! KNOCK!

Who's there?

Boo.

Boo who?

Don't cry - it's only a joke!

What goes click-clack-moo! Click-clack-moo!?

A cow using a typewriter!

What is a cow's favourite TV programme?

Moos at ten!

What's the best way of dealing with fleas?
Start from scratch!

What does a queen bee do when she burps?
Issues a royal pardon!

What was the most famous ant scientist?

Albert *Ant*-stein!

What do you give a sick ant?

Anti-biotics!

What do you call a hippo
with chicken pox?

A hippo-**spottymus**!

What do you call a Roman
Emperor with a cold?

Julius *Sneezer*!

What kind of vegetables
do maths teachers eat?

SQUARE ROOTS!

What sort of vegetables
do history teachers eat?

HAS-BEANS!

What do you call a snowman in the desert?

A puddle!

What do you call an eskimo's house with no toilet?

An ig!

What used to chase Softies in prehistoric times?

A Gnasher-saurus rex!

Sidney: Hey Danny, what's green and gets picked?
Danny: Errr...snot?
Sidney: No, apples!

Teacher: Danny, what came after the Stone Age and the Bronze Age?
Danny: The saus-age?!

What's the best way to catch a fish?

Get someone to throw one at you!

Are dolphins ever naughty by accident?

No - they always do it on porpoise!

Why did Dracula brush his teeth?

Because he had **bat** breath!

What is a vampire's favourite dog?

A bloodhound!

What goes Quick! Quick?
A duck with hiccups!

Why do gorillas have big nostrils?

Because they have big fingers!

Why do ducks have webbed feet?

So they can kick spiders!

What are invisible and smell of carrots?

Rabbit farts!

What is a grown-up?

Someone who has stopped growing at both ends and has started growing in the middle!

Have you heard the joke about the boy who slept with his head under the pillow?

When he woke up he found the Tooth Fairy had taken all his teeth!

What is grey and yellow and grey and yellow and grey and yellow?

An elephant rolling downhill with a daisy in its mouth!

What game do elephants play with ants?

Squash!

What do you call a boy who is a menace with a racket?

Dennis the Tennis!

Have you heard the joke about the tortoise who had his lunch money stolen by two snails?

When the police asked him if he could describe the snails he said, "No – it all happened so fast!"

Where do you take
a sick squid?
To a **doctor-pus**!

What's green and prickly?

A seasick hedgehog!

Why do humming birds hum?

Because they don't know the words!

How do you stop birds building nests?

Take away their tool belts!

Why did the chicken cross the road?

Because if the road crossed the chicken old ladies would trip over the bump!

What do you call a chicken that eats cement?

A brick-layer!